LEADING SERIES 2012

Introduction to leadership

Level 3

M3.10

ii

LEADING SERIES 2012

First edition August 2011

ISBN 9781 4453 8649 2

British Library Cataloguing-in-Publication Data
A catalogue record for this book is available
from the British Library

Published by

BPP Learning Media Ltd
BPP House, Aldine Place
London W12 8AA

www.bpp.com/learningmedia

www.bpp.com/ilm

Contents

iv

ILM Unit Specification M3.10

The Leading Series is validated by the Institute of Leadership and Management, one of the World's most prestigious awarding and membership bodies for team leaders and managers.

The Leading Series is written and regularly updated by specially selected authors and leadership practitioners. The challenge of leadership constantly changes and so do the Unit specifications set by ILM. The Leading Series is re-published annually and date-stamped to ensure you know you are up-to-date too.

This Leading Series workbook is tailored to satisfy the requirements of ILM Unit M3.10 *Introduction to leadership* (QCF unit ref F/501/3804).

Passing the Unit requires you to demonstrate a mixture of understanding and application.

Learning outcomes define the knowledge you will need to master. Assessment criteria describe the ways you must demonstrate you can apply this knowledge.

Guidance on the form of assessment to be completed will be provided by your Training Provider/Centre (and is described in the Qualification Specification documentation).

Learning outcomes (the learner will)		Assessment criteria (the learner can)
1 Understand leadership styles	1.1	Identify the factors that will influence their choice of leadership styles or behaviours in workplace situations
	1.2	Explain why these leadership styles or behaviours are likely to have a positive effect on individual and group behaviour
2 Understand leadership qualities and review own leadership qualities and potential	2.1	Assess own leadership behaviours and potential in the context of a particular leadership model and own organisation's working practices and culture, using feedback from others
	2.2	Describe appropriate actions to enhance own leadership behaviour in the context of the particular leadership model

Using this Leading Series workbook to help you pass this Unit

This workbook contains appropriate coverage of all the required knowledge for this Unit. You should:

- Read through the workbook ensuring you understand the knowledge being covered

- Read the illustrations to appreciate how these things can appear in the real world of leadership and management

- Complete the activities to help reinforce your knowledge and demonstrate that you have been reading and understanding the subject.

Applying what you have learned

The Unit Assessment criteria require you to show that you can apply your learning. Your Training Provider/Centre will guide you on how to demonstrate this.

The following activities can help you demonstrate application:

- Completing the activities in this workbook by writing in the spaces provided.

- Keeping a personal logbook to record your responses to the activities marked with this symbol of a red notebook

- Taking time to write your reflections on the knowledge you have been reading and filing these in your personal logbook. For example, where something you have read reminds you of something at work, or it has helped you understand and perform your job better.

- Finding documents from work, or articles from newspapers and the Internet, that demonstrate the things you have been reading about. File these in your personal logbook with an explanation of what they demonstrate and your reflections on them.

1 APPRECIATING THE ROLE OF THE LEADER

> "
>
> The key to successful leadership today is influence, not authority.
>
> Kenneth Blanchard (1939 – American management writer and academic)

Contents

1   Leadership v Management

Before we look at leadership in detail, it is important to differentiate between leadership and management.

ACTIVITY 1

GUIDE TIME 15 MINUTES

What is your personal view as to the difference between leadership and management?

_____

_____

_____

_____

_____

_____

_____

_____

_____

_____

_____

_____

_____

_____

_____

_____

_____

_____

_____

_____

_____

_____

_____

_____

_____

_____

_____

_____

_____

Leadership and management are distinct concepts but the words are often used as though they have the same meaning. This confusion may arise from the fact that sometimes the same person is employed to do the job of leader and manager.

A leader's job is to decide where their team is heading. A leader will set the ultimate aim, objective and goals for the team. They will then inspire and motivate the team to achieve the objectives set. This will involve reviewing progress and ensuring that the team is on course.

A manager's job is to set how the team will achieve the objectives set by the leader. They will overcome any problems the team encounter and decide how to deal with complexity.

A simple way of illustrating the difference between leader and manager is to use the example of a team who are set the goal of building a path from point A to point B.

The leader's job will be to:

- set the goal of building a path

- decide that the path will go from A to B

- inspire and motivate the team so that they want to build a path for their leader

- review progress and ensure that the team are building the path from A to B

The manager's job will be to:

- plan the project and decide budgets, pay and materials used

- implement plans and control the building of the path

- organise the team and delegate tasks to them

- overcome any problems e.g. trees blocking the route where the path is to be built.

Another way of differentiating a leader from a manager is to think of someone known as a world leader and think about what they did.

You will find that leaders are often great visionaries, and are able to inspire and motivate people in an exceptional way. They present their ideas to the world in a way that inspires their audience and creates commitment to the same ideals. They create the vision but do not set the detail of how their vision will be achieved. The details are decided by others. Other people plan and manage the work needed to achieve the leader's vision. The leader's job is to continue motivating and ensuring that their work is on course to achieve whatever objective or ideal they champion.

2 Leadership

There is a great deal of management writing on the subject of leadership. We will all be familiar with the argument as to whether leadership is an innate quality or whether it can be learned. It is now generally recognised that leadership, like any other management function, can be learned.

The role of the leader may be split into two main categories:

- Those associated with leader's responsibilities for organising and making sure the objective is completed; and

- Those associated with dealing with people.

ACTIVITY 2

GUIDE TIME 10 MINUTES

What sort of activity would you associate with objective-fulfilment (the first of the two categories defined)?

_____

_____

_____

_____

_____

_____

_____

_____

_____

_____

_____

_____

_____

_____

_____

_____

_____

_____

_____

_____

_____

_____

_____

You may have thought of the following:

- Liaising with other units or departments

- Planning the work of yourself and your team

- Ensuring the work of the team members is co-ordinated to prevent duplication and to make sure all are working to a common goal

- Identifying present and future problems and making decisive sound decisions to meet them

- Ensuring that the work being carried out is done in accordance with local policies

- Training your work force, particularly new members of staff

- Allocating resources to meet the demands placed upon them and, if necessary, determining which tasks need to take priority and which may have to be neglected if sufficient resources are not available.

ACTIVITY 3

GUIDE TIME 15 MINUTES

What sort of tasks would you associate with the people-related activities involved in leadership?

_____

_____

_____

_____

_____

_____

_____

_____

_____

_____

_____

_____

_____

_____

_____

_____

_____

_____

_____

_____

_____

_____

_____

_____

_____

_____

_____

_____

_____

_____

_____

_____

_____

_____

There are a variety of answers. The following are some of the more important you may have identified:

- Setting a clear model for others to follow.

- Conducting appraisals or routine reports and identifying training needs.

- Setting objectives and targets for your team and ensuring those objectives are achievable.

- Introducing new members to the team, whether they are new recruits or transferees from another department. Remember that a move to a workplace can present different problems particularly concerning local procedures.

- Providing a framework in which people can grow.

- Being aware of welfare matters, identifying those who may need counselling and providing help, or identifying where help can be found, in appropriate cases.

- Providing a sense of purpose and motivation to individuals and to the team as a whole.

- Dealing with matters of discipline, either informally or, if necessary, formally.

2 UNDERSTANDING THEORIES OF LEADERSHIP

> ❝❝
>
> You don't lead by hitting people over the head - that's assault, not leadership.
>
> Dwight D. Eisenhower (1890-1969: 34th President of the USA)

Contents

1 Trait theories

In the 1920s and 1930s, leadership research focused on trying to identify the traits that differentiated leaders from non-leaders. These early leadership theories were content theories, focusing on "what" an effective leader is, not on 'how' to effectively lead. The trait approach to understanding leadership assumes that certain physical, social, and personal characteristics are inherent in leaders.

Sets of traits and characteristics were identified to assist in selecting the right people to become leaders. Physical traits include being young to middle-aged, energetic, tall, and handsome. Social background traits include being educated at schools associated with the upper echelons of society and being socially prominent or upwardly mobile. Social characteristics include being charismatic, charming, tactful, popular, co-operative, and diplomatic. Personality traits include being self-confident, adaptable, assertive, and emotionally stable. Task-related characteristics include being driven to excel, accepting of responsibility, having initiative, and being results-oriented.

2 Behavioural theories

The behavioural theorists identified determinants of leadership so that people could be trained to be leaders. They developed training programmes to change managers' leadership behaviours and assumed that the best styles of leadership could be learned.

Theory X and Theory Y

Douglas McGregor described Theory X and Theory Y in his book, *The Human Side of Enterprise*. Theory X and Theory Y each represent different ways in which leaders view employees. Theory X managers believe that employees are motivated mainly by money, are lazy, unco-operative, and have poor work habits. Theory Y managers believe that subordinates work hard, are co-operative, and have positive attitudes.

Theory X is the traditional view of direction and control by managers.

- The average person has an inherent dislike of work and will avoid it if he or she can.

- Because of this dislike of work, most people must be controlled, directed, and threatened with punishment to ensure they expend adequate effort toward the achievement of organisational objectives.

- The average person prefers to be directed, wishes to avoid responsibility, and has relatively little ambition, but above all wants security.

Theory X leads naturally to an emphasis on the tactics of control - to procedures and techniques for telling people what to do, for determining whether they are doing it, and for administering rewards and punishment. Theory X explains the consequences of a particular managerial strategy. Because its assumptions are so unnecessarily limiting, it prevents managers from seeing the possibilities inherent in other managerial strategies. As long as the assumptions of Theory X influence managerial strategy, organisations will fail to discover, let alone utilise, the potentialities of the average person.

Theory Y is the view that individual and organisational goals can be integrated.

- The expenditures of physical and mental effort in work are as natural as play or rest.

- External control and the threat of punishment are not the only means for bringing out effort toward organisational objectives.

- Commitment to objectives is a function of the rewards associated with their achievement.

- The average human being learns, under proper conditions, not only to accept but also to seek responsibility.

- The capacity to exercise a relatively high degree of imagination, ingenuity, and creativity in the solution of organisational problems is widely, not narrowly, distributed in the population.

- Under the condition of modern industrial life, the intellectual potentialities of the average human being are only partially utilised.

Theory Y's purpose is to encourage integration, to create a situation in which an employee can achieve his or her own goals best by directing his or her efforts toward the objectives of the organisation. It is a deliberate attempt to link improvement in managerial competence with the satisfaction of higher level ego and self-actualisation needs. Theory Y leads to a preoccupation with the nature of relationships, with the creation of an environment which will encourage commitment to organisational objectives and which will provide opportunities for the maximum exercise of initiative, ingenuity, and self-direction in achieving them.

3 Contingency theories

Successful leaders must be able to identify clues in an environment and adapt their leadership behaviour to meet the needs of their team and of the particular situation. Even with good diagnostic skills, leaders may not be effective unless they can adapt their leadership style to meet the demands of their environment.

Fiedler's contingency model

Fred E. Fiedler's **contingency theory** suggests that there is no best way for managers to lead. Situations will create different leadership style requirements for a manager. The solution to a managerial situation is contingent on the factors that impinge on the situation. For example, in a highly routine environment where repetitive tasks are the norm, a certain leadership style may result in the best performance. The same leadership style may not work in a very dynamic environment.

Fiedler looked at three situations that could define the condition of a managerial task:

- Leader member relations: How well do the manager and the employees get along?

- The task structure: Is the job highly structured, fairly unstructured, or somewhere in between?

- Position power: How much authority does the manager possess?

Managers were rated as to whether they were relationship oriented or task oriented. Task oriented managers tend to do better in situations that have good leader-member relationships, structured tasks, and either weak or strong position power. They do well when the task is unstructured but positional power is strong. Also, they did well at the other end of the spectrum when the leader member relations were moderate to poor and the task was unstructured. Relationship oriented managers do better in all other situations. Thus, a given situation might call for a manager with a different style or a manager who could take on a different style for a different situation.

Another aspect of the contingency model theory is that the leader-member relations, task structure, and position power dictate a leader's situational control. Leader-member relations are the amount of loyalty, dependability, and support that the leader receives from employees. It is a measure of how the manager perceives they and the group of employees is getting along together. In a favourable relationship the manager has a high task structure and is able to reward and or punish employees without any problems. In an unfavourable relationship the task is usually unstructured and the leader possesses limited authority.

Hersey-Blanchard situational leadership

The Hersey-Blanchard situational leadership theory is based on the amount of direction (task behaviour) and amount of socio-emotional support (relationship behaviour) a leader must provide given the situation and the "level of maturity" of the followers.

Task behaviour is the extent to which the leader engages in spelling out the duties and responsibilities to an individual or group. This behaviour includes telling people what to do, how to do it, when to do it, where to do it, and who's to do it. In task behaviour the leader engages in one-way communication. Relationship behaviour is the extent to which the leader engages in two-way or multi-way communications. This includes listening, facilitating, and supportive behaviours. In relationship behaviour the leader engages in two-way communication by providing support. Maturity is the willingness and ability of a person to take responsibility for directing his or her own behaviour. People tend to have varying degrees of maturity, depending on the specific task, function, or objective that a leader is attempting to accomplish through their efforts.

We will look at this model in more detail later.

4 Transformational leadership

Transformational leadership blends the behavioural theories with a little of the trait theories. Transactional leaders, such as those identified in contingency theories, guide followers in the direction of established goals by clarifying role and task requirements. However, transformational leaders, who are charismatic and visionary, can inspire followers to transcend their own self-interest for the good of the organisation. Transformational leaders appeal to followers' ideals and moral values and inspire them to think about problems in new or different ways.

Leader behaviours used to influence followers include vision, framing, and impression management. Vision is the ability of the leader to bind people together with an idea. Framing is the process whereby leaders define the purpose of their movement in highly meaningful terms. Impression management is a leader's attempt to control the impressions that others form about the leader by practising behaviours that make the leader more attractive and appealing to others.

Research indicates that transformational, as compared to transactional, leadership is more strongly correlated with lower turnover rates, higher productivity, and higher employee satisfaction.

A transformational leader instils feelings of confidence, admiration and commitment in the followers. He or she is charismatic, creating a special bond with followers, articulating a vision with which the followers identify and for which they are willing to work. Each follower is coached, advised, and delegated some authority. The transformational leader stimulates followers intellectually, arousing them to develop new ways to think about problems. The leader uses contingent rewards to positively reinforce performances that are consistent with the leader's wishes. Management is by exception. The leader takes initiative only when there are problems and is not actively involved when things are going well. The transformational leader commits people to action and converts followers into leaders.

Transformational leaders are relevant to today's workplace because they are flexible and innovative. While it is important to have leaders with the appropriate orientation defining tasks and managing interrelationships, it is even more important to have leaders who can bring organisations into futures they have not yet imagined. Transformational leadership is the essence of creating and sustaining competitive advantage.

5 | Leadership styles

One of the best known descriptions of leadership styles came from Tannenbaum and Schmidt and was published in '*How to choose a leadership pattern*' (1973). They looked at the balance between the use of authority by the leader and the extent to which the 'subordinate' was allowed to make, or be involved in, the decision making process.

6 | Tannenbaum and Schmidt's continuum

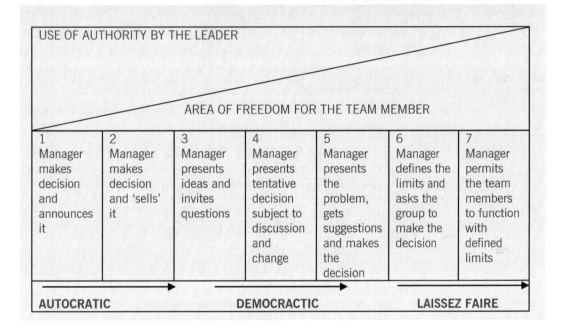

USE OF AUTHORITY BY THE LEADER						
AREA OF FREEDOM FOR THE TEAM MEMBER						
1 Manager makes decision and announces it	2 Manager makes decision and 'sells' it	3 Manager presents ideas and invites questions	4 Manager presents tentative decision subject to discussion and change	5 Manager presents the problem, gets suggestions and makes the decision	6 Manager defines the limits and asks the group to make the decision	7 Manager permits the team members to function with defined limits
AUTOCRATIC		DEMOCRACTIC			LAISSEZ FAIRE	

An overview of the continuum

Leaders who operate at the left of the continuum are commonly referred to as 'autocratic' leaders.

These leaders tend to keep total power in their control, viewing their subordinates as being incapable of original or constructive thought. They could be considered, for want of a better word, a dictator.

Those that work in the centre area of the continuum are often referred to as 'democratic' leaders.

These leaders tend to co-ordinate the work of the team.

Those that operate at the right of the continuum are referred to as 'laissez-faire' leaders. It could be argued that these are not really leaders at all as they tend to let everyone make their own decisions and do things their way.

In reality, leaders should adopt different styles at different times. When there is a crisis, then it is probably necessary for the leader to take total control and use an autocratic style. For more general situations, then maybe a more democratic style may be appropriate. It is probably only in rare situations that a laissez-faire approach should be adopted.

What we are really saying is that the style of leadership needs to vary from time to time. In times of crises an autocratic style may be necessary - there is not time to discuss options and obtain group decisions. On other occasions a democratic style may be more appropriate and productive.

The Tannenbaum and Schmidt Continuum is a simple model which shows the relationship between the level of freedom that a manager chooses to give to a team, and the level of authority used by the manager. As the team's freedom is increased, so the manager's authority decreases. This is a positive way for both teams and managers to develop. While the Tannenbaum and Schmidt model concerns delegated freedom to a group, the principle of being able to apply different levels of delegated freedom closely relates to the 'seven levels of delegation'. As a manager, one of your responsibilities is to develop your team. You should delegate and ask a team to make its own decisions to varying degrees according to their abilities. There is a rising scale of levels of delegated freedom that you can use when working with your team.

Over time, a manager should aim to take the team from one end to the other, up the scale, at which point you should also aim to have developed one or a number of potential successors from within your team to take over from you. This process can take a year or two, or even longer, so be patient, explain what you're doing, and be aware constantly of how your team is responding and developing.

When examining and applying the Tannenbaum and Schmidt principles, it is extremely important to remember:

- Irrespective of the amount of responsibility and freedom delegated by a manager to a team, the manager retains accountability for any catastrophic problems that result.

- Delegating freedom and decision-making responsibility to a team absolutely does not absolve the manager of accountability. That is why delegating, whether to teams or individuals, requires a very grown-up manager.

- If everything goes well, the team must get the credit; if it all goes horribly wrong, the manager must take the blame. This is entirely fair, because the manager is ultimately responsible for judging the seriousness of any given situation - including the risks entailed - and the level of freedom that can safely be granted to the team to deal with it. This is not strictly part of the Tannenbaum and Schmidt Continuum, but it is vital to apply this philosophy or the model weakened, or is or may back-fire.

Here are the Tannenbaum and Schmidt Continuum levels of delegated freedom, with some added explanation that should make it easier to understand and apply the theory.

1. The manager decides and announces the decision.

   The manager reviews options in light of aims, issues, priorities, timescale, and so on then decides the action and informs the team of the decision. The manager will probably have considered how the team will react, but the team plays no active part in making the decision. The team may well perceive that the manager has not considered the team's welfare at all. This is seen by the team as a purely task-based decision.

2. The manager decides and then 'sells' the decision to the group.

   The manager makes the decision as in 1 above, and then explains reasons for the decision to the team, particularly the positive benefits that the team will enjoy from the decision. In so doing the manager is seen by the team to recognise the team's importance, and to have some concern for the team.

3. The manager presents the decision with background ideas and invites questions.

The manager presents the decision along with some of the background which led to the decision. The team is invited to ask questions and discuss with the manager the rationale behind the decision, which enables the team to understand and accept or agree with the decision more easily than in 1 and 2 above. This more participative and involving approach enables the team to appreciate the issues and reasons for the decision, and the implications of all the options. This will have a more motivational approach than 1 or 2 because of the higher level of team involvement and discussion.

4. The manager suggests a provisional decision and invites discussion about it.

The manager discusses and reviews the provisional decision with the team on the basis that the manager will take on board the views and then finally decide. This enables the team to have some real influence over the shape of the manager's final decision. This also acknowledges that the team has something to contribute to the decision-making process, which is more involving and therefore motivating than the previous level.

5. The manager presents the situation or problem, gets suggestions, and then decides.

The manager presents the situation, and maybe some options, to the team. The team is encouraged and expected to offer ideas and additional options, and discuss implications of each possible course of action. The manager then decides which option to take. This level is one of high and specific involvement for the team, and is appropriate particularly when the team has more detailed knowledge or experience of the issues than the manager. Being high-involvement and high-influence for the team this level provides more motivation and freedom than any previous level.

6. The manager explains the situation, defines the parameters and asks the team to decide.

At this level the manager has effectively delegated responsibility for the decision to the team, albeit within the manager's stated limits. The manager may or may not choose to be a part of the team which decides. While this level appears to gives a huge responsibility to the team, the manager can control the risk and outcomes to an extent, according to the constraints that he stipulates. This level is more motivational than any previous, and requires a mature team for any serious situation or problem. (Remember that the team must get the credit for all the positive outcomes from the decision, while the manager remains accountable for any resulting problems or disasters. This isn't strictly included in the original Tannenbaum and Schmidt definitions, but it needs pointing out because it's such an important aspect of delegating and motivating, and leadership.)

7. The manager allows the team to identify the problem, develop the options and decide on the action, within the manager's defined limits.

This is obviously an extreme level of freedom, whereby the team is effectively doing what the manager did in level 1. The team is given responsibility for identifying and analysing the situation or problem; the process for resolving it; developing and assessing options; evaluating implications, and then deciding on and implementing a course of action. The manager also states in advance that he/she will support the decision and help the team implement it. The manager may or may not be part of the team, and if so then he/she has no more authority than anyone else in the team. The only constraints and parameters for the team are the ones that the manager had imposed on him from above. (Again, the manager retains accountability for any resulting disasters, while the team must get the credit for all successes.) This level is potentially the most motivational of all, but also potentially the most disastrous. Not surprisingly the team must be mature and competent, and capable of acting at what is a genuinely strategic decision-making level.

ACTIVITY 4

GUIDE TIME 20 MINUTES

What is the most common 'style' of leadership in your team and how does this affect the team members?

Ask other team members how they feel about it when you are thinking of your answer.

Later you will be asked to do a more comprehensive analysis in the form of a leadership styles questionnaires.

You response will depend on your own circumstances, but in essence you may have found that if the style of leadership tends towards the autocratic, that people do not feel involved or valued and may get frustrated. Also that when the leader is absent, there is a reluctance to take decisions. Conversely, if the style tends towards the laissez-faire, that there is a lack of direction and confusion. If the style is normally in the democratic range, people feel that they know what is expected, that their opinions count, that they own the problems and solutions and feel generally more involved in what is going on.

ACTIVITY 5

GUIDE TIME 120 MINUTES

Team leadership styles

Purpose

The purpose of this diagnostic activity is to help you identify your leadership style as a team leader and explore the implications of this.

Instructions

Consider the list of statements below, in relation to yourself as a team leader, and indicate how often you do the things described. Use the following scale:

1. Never

2. Hardly ever

3. Sometimes

4. Most of the time

5. Always

You should write your responses in column A. In the other columns you can record the views of your team members. To do this photocopy the second questionnaire and ask your team members to complete it. Once they have, transfer their scores to the main questionnaire.

AS A TEAM LEADER I	A	B	C	D	E	F	G	H	I
1. Make all the decisions									
2. Issue agreed statements									
3. Support the team's position									
4. Am happy with any decision									
5. Tells the team only what they need to know									
6. Exercise control through other people									
7. Seek trust and respect from team members									
8. Allow the team to make their own decisions									
9. Issue orders									
10. Negotiate standards									
11. Am prepared to change my position if challenged									
12. Assume the team will find out what they need to know									
13. Operate fairly rigid systems and procedures									

LEADING SERIES 2012

AS A TEAM LEADER I	A	B	C	D	E	F	G	H	I
14. Am prepared to negotiate decisions									
15. Help the team to identify appropriate standards									
16. Avoid change at all costs									
17. Initiate necessary changes									
18. Ask the team what they want to know									
19. Help the team to learn from mistakes									
20. Keep my work separate from team members									
21. Keep a strong control of activities									
22. Try to prevent mistakes happening									
23. Provide the information for the team to make decisions									
24. Assume the team trust me									
25. Defend my position strongly									
26. Follow up on delegated work									
27. Work with team members									
28. Allow a great deal of team autonomy									
29. Like to make decisions that will stick									
30. Seek obedience									
31. Pass on everything I know									
32. Generally accept team members' standards									
33. Delegate only when there is no alternative									
34. Inform the team of the reasons for change									
35. Help the team to reach decisions									
36. Ask the team how they want to go about achieving things									
37. Keep up a high pressure of work									
38. Develop rules and guidelines									
39. Identify sources of conflict									

AS A TEAM LEADER I	A	B	C	D	E	F	G	H	I
40. Sort out mistakes if they cause a problem									
41. Try to prevent conflict occurring									
42. Seek workable decisions									
43. Delegate whenever possible									
44. Let the team work out what is required									
45. Expect obedience									
46. Negotiate solutions to conflict									
47. Do not expect people to follow routine									
48. Ignore any opposing views									
49. Find out who is responsible, when things go wrong									
50. Discuss any opposing views									
51. Encourage the team to develop its own momentum									
52. Let the team sort out conflict									
53. Set high standards									
54. Accept a fair day's work									
55. Encourage us to go in new directions									
56. Allow the team to decide its own routines									

Now enter your scores against the statements as they are numbered below and add up each column.

DIRECTING	NEGOTIATING	FACILITATING	LAISSEZ-FAIRE
1	2	3	4
5	6	7	8
9	10	11	12
13	14	15	16
17	18	19	20
21	22	23	24
25	26	27	28
29	30	31	32

LEADING SERIES 2012

DIRECTING	NEGOTIATING	FACILITATING	LAISSEZ-FAIRE
33	34	35	36
37	38	39	40
41	42	43	44
45	46	47	48
49	50	51	52
53	54	55	56

The questionnaire highlights four leadership styles.

Directing - Where the leader makes all the decisions and tells people what to do. To adopt this style the leader needs to be assertive, prepared to disagree with people and be extremely knowledgeable about all situations in which the team might find itself. Useful in high risk roles.

Negotiating - Where the leader seeks to achieve consensus on what should be done, how it should be done and the resources needed. Involves a great deal of consultation and negotiation. The leader will need political and social skills. Particularly useful where there is scope for compromise.

Facilitating - Where the leader seeks to provide support, facilities, resources and expertise and encourages team members to make their own decisions. The leader effectively becomes a coach and "cheer leader". High level personal and social skills are required for this work. Useful when performing a consultancy role.

Laissez-faire - Where the leader has very little personal involvement and leaves the team to get on with it. This can be a risky approach. Works best with highly skilled, well integrated teams. It often means that the leader becomes more of a figurehead. Useful with established and professional teams.

The higher your score in each column, the more you tend towards this style of leadership.

Looking at this from your own perspective alone can be misleading, so use the questionnaire below (photocopy the pages) and ask your team members or colleagues to complete it.

Photocopy

Team leadership styles team member questionnaire

Purpose

The purpose of this diagnostic activity is to help your team leader identify his/her leadership style as a team leader and explore the implications of this.

Instructions

Consider the list of statements below, in relation to your team leader, and indicate how often he/she does the things described. Use the following scale:

1. Never

2. Hardly ever

3. Sometimes

4. Most of the time

5. Always

You should write your responses your responses in column A. When you have completed the questionnaire, please return it to the team leader so that the results can be collated.

MY TEAM LEADER ...	A
1. Makes all the decisions	
2. Issues agreed statements	
3. Supports the team's position	
4. Is happy with any decision	
5. Tells the team only what they need to know	
6. Exercises control through other people	
7. Seeks trust and respect from team members	
8. Allows the team to make their own decisions	
9. Issues orders	
10. Negotiates standards	
11. Is prepared to change his/her position if challenged	
12. Assumes we will find out what we need to know	
13. Operates fairly rigid systems and procedures	
14. Is prepared to negotiate decisions	
15. Helps the team to identify appropriate standards	
16. Avoids change at all costs	
17. Initiates necessary changes	
18. Asks the team what we want to know	

MY TEAM LEADER ...	A
19. Help the team to learn from mistakes	
20. Keeps his/her work separate from team members	
21. Keeps a strong control of activities	
22. Ties to prevent mistakes happening	
23. Provides the information for the team to make decision	
24. Assumes the team trusts his/her	
25. Defends his/her position strongly	
26. Follows up on delegated work	
27. Works with team members	
28. Allows a great deal of team autonomy	
29. Likes to make decisions that will stick	
30. Seeks obedience	
31. Passes on everything he/she knows	
32. Generally accepts team members' standards	
33. Delegates only when there is no alternative	
34. Informs the team of the reasons for change	
35. Helps the team to reach decisions	
36. Asks the team how they want to go about achieving things	
37. Keeps up a high pressure of work	
38. Develops rules and guidelines	
39. Identifies the source of conflict	
40. Sorts out mistakes if they cause a problem	
41. Tries to prevent conflict occurring	
42. Seeks workable decisions	
43. Delegates whenever possible	
44. Lets the team work out what is required	
45. Expects obedience	
46. Negotiates solutions to conflict	
47. Does not expect people to follow routine	
48. Ignores any opposing views	
49. Finds out who is responsible, when things go wrong	
50. Discusses any opposing views	
51. Encourages the team to develop its own momentum	
52. Lets the team sort out conflict	

MY TEAM LEADER ...	A
53. Sets high standards	
54. Accepts a fair day's work	
55. Encourages us to go in new directions	
56. Allows the team to decide its own routines	

Now enter your scores against the statements as they are numbered below and add up each column.

1	2	3	4
5	6	7	8
9	10	11	12
13	14	15	16
17	18	19	20
21	22	23	24
25	26	27	28
29	30	31	32
33	34	35	36
37	38	39	40
41	42	43	44
45	46	47	48
49	50	51	52
53	54	55	56

22

ACTIVITY 6

GUIDE TIME 15 MINUTES

Compare the results from your own questionnaire with those of your team members or colleagues. What differences are there and what does this tell you?

_____

_____

_____

_____

_____

_____

_____

_____

_____

_____

_____

_____

_____

3 USING THE TECHNIQUES OF LEADERSHIP

> " A leader leads by example, whether he intends to or not.
>
> Anonymous

Contents

1 Situational leadership

Kenneth Blanchard took another approach when he looked at 'situational leadership' by considering leadership in terms of 'directive behaviour' and 'supportive behaviour'.

By combining high and low levels of each type of behaviour we progress towards four distinct styles of leadership:

DIRECTING	The leader provides specific instructions and closely supervises task accomplishment.
COACHING	The leader continues to direct and closely supervise task accomplishment, but also explains decisions, solicits suggestions and supports progress.
SUPPORTING	The leader facilitates and supports subordinates' efforts towards task accomplishment and shares responsibility for decision making with them.
DELEGATING	The leader turns over responsibility for decision making and problem solving to subordinates.

The choice of 'style' will depend on the individual, or group of individuals, being led. These can be considered in four broad combinations that may reflect the stage of development of those being led:

LOW COMPETENCE * HIGH COMMITMENT	SOME COMPETENCE * LOW COMMITMENT	HIGH COMPETENCE * VARIABLE COMMITMENT	HIGH COMPETENCE * HIGH COMMITMENT
D1	D2	D3	D4
DEVELOPING		→	DEVELOPED

The diagram above illustrates these levels.

At an early stage of development competence is likely to be low but often there is generally a high level of commitment due to the excitement of a new task and the opportunity of learning something new.

As the competence levels increase, commitment tends to drop, as the person(s) become(s) aware of just what the task requires and how much more needs to be learned.

When the knowledge level is high and the skills have been developed, commitment will tend to vary due to the lack of confidence or motivation that will result from any number of factors.

The last level of development comes with a confident and self-motivated individual, fully developed in terms of knowledge and skill.

When you consider these stages, it is not unreasonable to suggest an appropriate leadership style for each.

DEVELOPMENT LEVEL	APPROPRIATE LEADERSHIP STYLE
D1 LOW COMPETENCE * HIGH COMMITMENT	S1 DIRECTING Structure, control and supervise

DEVELOPMENT LEVEL	APPROPRIATE LEADERSHIP STYLE
D2 SOME COMPETENCE * LOW COMMITMENT	S2 COACHING Direct and support
D3 HIGH COMPETENCE * VARIABLE COMMITMENT	S3 SUPPORTING Praise, listen and facilitate
D4 HIGH COMPETENCE * HIGH COMMITMENT	S4 DELEGATING Turn over responsibility for day-to-day decision making

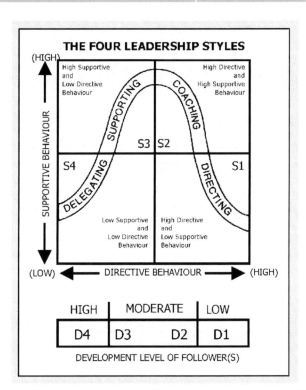

A **Directing Style** is for people who lack competence but are enthusiastic and committed. They need direction and supervision to get them started.

A **Coaching Style** is for people who have some competence but lack commitment. They need direction and supervision because they are still relatively inexperienced. They also need support and praise to build their self-esteem, and involvement in decision making to restore their commitment.

A **Supporting Style** is for people who have competence but lack confidence or motivation. They do not need much direction because of their skills but good support is necessary to boost their confidence and motivation.

A **Delegating Style** is for people who have both competence and commitment. They are able and willing to work on a task or project by themselves with little supervision or support.

The diagram has been modified to show this complex relationship. The four styles are shown as an open curve to indicate that movement from one style to another can and probably will occur. This is shown above the development levels to indicate normal relationships.

2 Power, authority and influence

To perform your role as a manager, you have to have a degree of power, authority and influence over those you are responsible for.

The whole question of where a manager or leader obtains their 'power' to cause compliance is a complex issue.

In the 1960s and 1970s the concept of the 'chain of command' was a key issue in organisational design. This chain of command relied on three concepts: authority, responsibility and unity of command.

The idea was that the authority conferred on a holder of a certain position provided the right to issue orders and expect them to be obeyed. Breach of this was a punishable offence. The right to give orders, however, also placed a responsibility on the office holder to perform as required and to exercise their authority properly. It was also seen to be necessary that there was unity in the chain of command so that each manager had one superior to whom they were responsible.

More recently the notion of power has been examined and divided into five sources of power – legitimate, coercive, reward, expert and referent.

Legitimate power is the same as authority. It results from an individual's position in the hierarchy. It relies on the acceptance of that authority by others in the organisation.

Coercive power is exercised using fear as its source. The exercise of this form of power relies on the fear of negative results that arise through failure to comply. Most managers have some source of coercive power in their ability to suspend, or even dismiss employees or impose demotion or some other form of punishment. Coercive power, of course, is not unique to a manager. A subordinate may be in a position to exercise coercive power against a manager because of knowledge they may hold about the manager's behaviour!

Reward power is straightforward. It results from the ability to reward those who comply. The reward can be anything from some form of remuneration to praise, friendship, allocation of interesting work and many other factors.

Expert power results from the influence wielded through the holder's expertise, skill or knowledge. This has become an increasingly potent source of power in the modern organisation.

Referent power results from the holding of desirable resources or personal traits. It develops from an admiration of the holder.

ACTIVITY 7

GUIDE TIME 15 MINUTES

To what extent do the sources of power outlined play a part in the authority of managers within your organisation?

3 Trust

What we have not included, but is critical, is the whole issue of respect and trust. You will gain these from your team members through open and honest communication and through your own behaviour.

ACTIVITY 8

GUIDE TIME 10 MINUTES

What factors do you think helps your team members trust you?

_____

_____

_____

_____

_____

_____

_____

_____

_____

_____

_____

_____

_____

_____

_____

_____

_____

_____

_____

_____

Overall, trust is the belief in the integrity, character and ability of a leader.

It can be argued that there are five dimensions that make up the concept of trust:

- Integrity – honesty and truthfulness

- Competence – technical and interpersonal knowledge and skill

- Consistency – reliability, predictability and good judgement in handling situations

- Loyalty – willingness to protect and save face for a person

- Openness – willingness to share ideas and information freely.

How does a team leader build trust?

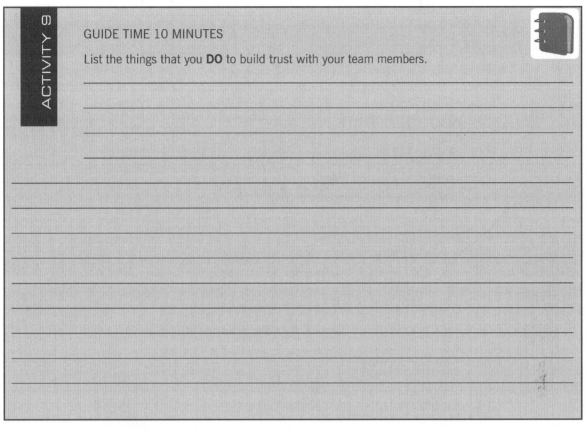

Here are some suggestions:

Practise openness – mistrust comes from what people know, just as much as from what they don't know. Openness leads to confidence and trust. Keep people informed, make the criteria you use to make decisions clear, explain your rationale for decisions and be candid about problems. Fully disclose relevant information.

Be fair – before you make decisions or take action, consider how people will perceive your actions in terms of objectivity and fairness. Give credit where it is due and be impartial in your appraisals.

Speak your feelings – if you only convey hard facts you come across as cold, distant and uncaring. If you share your feelings, others will see you as a real human being.

Tell the truth – as honesty is critical to credibility you must be seen as someone who tells the truth. People tend to be more tolerant of learning something negative than finding out that their leader has lied to them.

Show consistency – people like predictability. Mistrust comes from not knowing what to expect. Think about your values and beliefs and let them guide your decisions and actions.

Fulfil your promises – people will trust someone who is dependable. Make sure you keep your word and fulfil promises that you make.

Maintain confidences – people trust those that are discreet and on whom they can rely.

Demonstrate competence – develop the admiration and respect of others by demonstrating technical and professional ability. Pay particular attention to developing and practising effective communication, negotiation and other interpersonal skills.

How is a high level of trust achieved? Through kept promises!

Here is how Jon R. Katzenbach and Douglas K. Smith explain it in their book *'The Wisdom of Teams'*.

'At its core, team accountability is about the sincere promises we make to ourselves and others, promises that underpin two critical aspects of effective teams: commitment and trust. By promising to hold ourselves accountable to the team's goals, we each earn the right to express our own views about all aspects of the team's effort and to have our views receive a fair and constructive hearing. By following through on such a promise we preserve and extend the trust upon which any team must be built.'

We will end this workbook with another questionnaire you can use to rate yourself as a leader. Be as honest as you can with your answers.

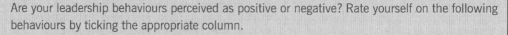

ACTIVITY 10

GUIDE TIME 30 MINUTES

How do you rate as a leader?

Adapted from: www.attitudeworks.com.au

Are your leadership behaviours perceived as positive or negative? Rate yourself on the following behaviours by ticking the appropriate column.

	ALWAYS	ALMOST ALWAYS	SOMETIMES	ALMOST NEVER	NEVER
I give honest and objective feedback at the appropriate time					
I respond to problems with understanding and help					
I show support for team member's actions and decisions					
I help alleviate stressful situations for team members					
I socialise with team members where appropriate					
I keep team members informed about stressful or challenging situations					
I address team members' negative feelings					
I disclose personal information to team members where appropriate					
I recognise good work privately					
I recognise good work publicly					
I ask team members for their ideas and opinions					

	ALWAYS	ALMOST ALWAYS	SOMETIMES	ALMOST NEVER	NEVER
I act on team members' ideas or suggestions					
I monitor the progress of a project rather than making individuals feel personally monitored					
I frequently report my own progress to the team					
I actively sell a project to other parts of the organisation					
I gather external information to help the team generate new ideas					
I outline project objectives clearly					
I ask team members how they are **feeling** about their work					
I actively listen to team members					
It is easy for team members to approach me					
I provide team members with clear information about their roles and responsibilities					
I hold regular meetings to gain feedback from the team about their problems and ideas					

Your rating:

Your strengths are those items you answered 'Always' or 'Almost Always'. If you answered 'Never' or 'Almost Never' to any of the items, we would suggest you test how important these are with your team. If your team thinks they are important, focus on developing these behaviours, as these may be hindering your ability to lead your team.

If you scored poorly, don't be too distraught – self-awareness is the first step to changing your behaviour.

Now consider how your team would rate you, or better still -ask your team to rate you on the above dimensions. Would your team's rating be consistent with your own rating? If not, why not? Where are the gaps?

ACTIVITY 11

GUIDE TIME 30 MINUTES

Using your evaluation of yourself and the discrepancies between how you rate yourself and how your team rates you, identify one aspect at a time that you could work on. With this one aspect, identify:

What's stopping you from doing it now?

Why has this stopped you?

What might happen if you start to improve this?

How might this benefit the team and yourself?

What specific steps could you put in place to start changing this?

When will you start doing this?

How will you measure your progress?

What might get in the way to hinder you from making this change? Who could give you some feedback on your progress?

Passing this Unit can contribute to you receiving one of the following ILM Vocationally Related Qualifications (VRQ).

ILM Level 3 Award in Effective Management
ILM Level 3 Award in First Line Management
ILM Level 3 Award in Leadership
ILM Level 3 Award in Leadership and Management Skills
ILM Level 3 Certificate in Effective Management
ILM Level 3 Certificate in First Line Management
ILM Level 3 Certificate in Leadership
ILM Level 3 Certificate in Leadership and Management Skills
ILM Level 3 Certificate in Managing Innovation and Change in the Workplace
ILM Level 3 Diploma in First Line Management
ILM Level 3 Diploma in Leadership and Management
ILM Level 4 Award in Leadership
ILM Level 4 Certificate in Leadership and Management Skills
ILM Level 4 Certificate in Management
ILM Level 4 Diploma in Leadership and Management
ILM Level 4 Diploma in Management
ILM Level 4 Extended Diploma in Leadership and Management
ILM Level 3 Extended Diploma in Management

There is a Leading Series Workbook for the remaining Units needed to complete these ILM Qualifications

Full details of ILM Qualifications can be found at www.i-l.m.com